**Gateshead** *Council*

C000072086

Due for Return	Due for Return	Due for Return

Visit us at:

www.gateshead.gov.uk/books

Tel: 0191 433 8400

C1 830977 60

Also by Joy Howard

SECOND BITE
(with Hilary J Murray and Gina Shaw)

A TWIST OF MALICE (ed)

EXIT MOONSHINE

CRACKING ON (ed)

NO SPACE BUT THEIR OWN (ed)

GET ME OUT OF HERE!

Poems for Trying Circumstances

Edited by Joy Howard

First published in 2011 by Grey Hen Press
PO Box 450
Keighley
West Yorkshire
BD22 9WS
www.greyhenpress.com

ISBN 978-0-9552952-3-2

Printed by GB Print & Design, Loughborough, Leicestershire LE11 1LE

Thanks are due to all the contributors, who have made the process of compiling this book such a pleasure. And a nod to Ant and Dec.

Poetry is the record of the best and happiest moments of the best and happiest minds.

Shelley

Poetry is a way of taking life by the throat.

Robert Frost

Preface

The inspiration for this book came from my reading that *'poetry was of profound importance in the northern world, playing a role similar to the mass media of today'*.* How far removed is that from our own world. Now you have to sign up for ordeals by jungle to enhance your celebrity status. Wouldn't it be nice to bring back honour and renown without benefit of mudslides and creepie-crawlies?

So here is a collection of poems that bypasses bush tucker trials and offers instead poetic responses to the everyday struggles that can bog us down and prevent us connecting with our inner Milton or Shakespeare. I hope all poets and lovers of poetry will enjoy sharing these teeth-grinding experiences of the frustration, exasperation and general outrage with so much that constitutes modern life. Next stop: the ground-breaking epic, the rhymed sestina and the sonnet sequence we were working on before being rudely interrupted.

Joy Howard

* R. Rudgley: 'Ancient Blueprints in the Modern Mind', *Pagan Resurrection*.

Contents

Primo

Nobody's Darlings

Location, Location

Speaking in Tongues

Travelling Blight

Home Sweet Home

Poetic Licence

All Worked Up

Great Escapes

Finale

The Poets   133

Index of Poets   139

Acknowledgements   141

Primo

Get Me In

I'm lost on the bleak Saturday campus
so I ask Security for directions

'Poetry?' he says, 'you want *POETRY*?'
and he draws himself back horrified

as though I'm one of those long-leggedy
beasties that scribbles itself across the carpet

Gina Shaw

Nobody's Darlings

Happy Hour at the Pig and Polecat

Crammed in, as Jason says,
like ferrets in a posing-pouch
you couldn't push a sausage-stick
between us, and old Nick,
that's our landlord,
a terrific bloke,
the twenty stone bastard,
he's just back,
from his usual trip
in Thailand – God,
he makes us laugh,
you should hear the one
about these two girls –
he swears they're no more
than twelve or thirteen
if they're a day but a pair
of real little goers
and gagging for it
apparently –
well, between them
they give him the full works
a right going over,
a Bangkok sandwich
he called it, makes you sweat
even to think of it
so next year
we'll be going with him –
yeah, the Pub outing –
well wicked.

Angela Kirby

Blind Date

I'm sweet. I'm petite. I can rave. I can groove.
Hung-over just slightly but really don't show it.
This little red dress is as snug as a glove.
I just hope they don't fix me up with a poet.

Mascara. Tiara. Blusher. High heels.
A wild oat remaining and ready to sow it.
Let's hope he'll have money. Let's hope he'll have *wheels*.
But let me not end up in bed with a poet.

No noting, no quoting, no 'wrote you a poem',
no armed-with-own-trumpet and desperate to blow it;
no name-dropping (Armitage? met him? I *know* him).
Dear God, please remember: I don't want a poet.

Helena Nelson

A Ride Home with the Hypnotherapist

She says she can tell I'm spiritual,
asks if my husband's spiritual too
and when I say not really enquires
How then does it work? It just does.

She works a lot with weight loss clients
but I think she says weightless
and picture her jumping up and down,
anchoring them to a safe surface.

She says as I'm so spiritual if I like
she'll do regression to a previous life
for free and how would I feel about that?
I say *terrified.*

She asks am I afraid of death,
do I really think I'd no longer exist
so I tell her about my near death experience
and she's on the edge of her seat.

I think in a previous life
she was a nervous, rather clumsy pony
a bit like the ones in the Thelwell cartoons
but I don't mention this.

Carole Bromley

What the Harassed Woman Wished She'd Replied to the Bus Driver Who Said:

Hey ducky, why do you women always look so exhausted
when all you've done is go shopping?

Well, drakey, I just wouldn't know.
I don't have that much time for shopping, see.
Today, I caught a very early train
to meet a Chief Exec with super brain
and just to fill the 2-hour trip
I made 8 calls, 5 deals, then had a power kip.
That's *after* I had left the bloke and kids times 2
set up and ready with instructions what to do
to get them through another tricky day.
So, in my meeting (having phoned them on the way),
I gave a presentation, stunned the Chief Exec,
and left the partners looking somewhat wrecked,
employing my advanced negotiation skills,
and special expertise in looks that kill,
and pulled off quite a stunning coup,
still managing to leave for half past 2.

So here I am, back off the London train
and managing to dodge the pouring rain,
and in this bag which you assumed was full
of nappies, pot pourri and balls of wool,
mascara, perfume, knickers or hair lacquer
is, in fact, a contract worth a hundred thousand smackers.

So, now we've got that absolutely clear
just put your little stick in gear
and drive me home on your *enormous*
bus.

Cathy Grindrod

Unfair to Snails

There is nothing in the animal kingdom
to compare her to; except perhaps
some silent, slithering snail, leaving
a trail of slime for you to slip on.
She looks so harmless, fragile even,
tucked away inside her delicate shell.
You must be careful where you tread,
in case by accident you crush her.

But when she senses you aren't looking,
she'll poke her head out, and turn on you
those baleful eyes, those vicious horns.

Rosemary McLeish

Off Her Trolley

She stormed through Tesco's car-park,
an avenging Boadicea,
knives scything from her wayward
trolley wheels. 'So they sent me,'
she roared to her cowering companion,
'to the reality clinic'…

And you thought *I* had problems…

Lyn Moir

A TV Presenter Attempts to Explain Modern Classical Music

Light shone on a long man
perched at
the side of a huge bell.

He waved his arms
like wings on a brazen angel.
'This iron mouth
has more than one song,
endless sounds
run through its metal fibres,
live in its shell.'

Oh the metallurgy
of his metaphor,
the toll of his telling
the tell of his tolling.

Ecstacies
rolled through his words,
I felt the swell
in the gong at the earth's core,

cacophony fell.

Isobel Thrilling

Firing Day

Far off, the guns sound
like laundry flapping. Listen
to the peaceful guns.

Up on the high fell
nothing waves or warns except
a red flag or two.

There are peregrine,
dunlin it's said and black grouse
where nobody walks.

Sheep don't disturb them.
Live ammo in the heather
makes no stumbling block.

We value greatly,
the Colonel writes, our record
of conservation.

(He carries very
powerful binoculars
like a gamekeeper.

He counts the number
of angels perched on the pin
of a ripe grenade.)

M R Peacocke

A Letter to the Council

I received your letter this morning
There are procedures you say
and I should have informed you,
which I have on several occasions
and been discouraged by your response.
Remember how you received my plans
for a proposed extension. 'Overlooking,'
you said and the same went for the Italian
balcony. Now you complain about something
I've taken down! Yes I've read the terms
of the lease and it mentions landscaping
which, in a sense, is what I have done.
I thought I was doing a good turn
removing that tree. It creaked all night
(noise nuisance I think you'll find),
harboured crows and grey squirrels,
oozed a disgusting sap and shed leaves
all over the path. Worse still
it was stealing my light. I had no idea
it was something you wished to conserve.
As for the damage, I agree it would have been
better if it had landed somewhere else
(I think I know who complained).
When I pulled on the rope, I thought
the angle was spot on but I'm not Pythagoras
and there was no-one around when it fell
so no harm done apart from the fence.
I trust you will take this into consideration
when assessing my case.

Yours truly

Ruth Smith

Balloons and Stripy Trousers

I love those nineteen sixties hangover towns
their middleclass peoples, plotting revolutions,
community spirit and all. Without exception
you'll find them ensconced in somewhere agreeably ancient
where cottages tumble down hills. I love their affronted
we-don't-like-the-twentyfirst-century air,
their fluting insistent voices. It seems
whoever you meet has attended a private school
is in, or just out of, therapy
and paints, or writes, or makes
those indestructible bargelike leathertop shoes
in various shades of neon. I love
their innocence, born of always being right,
their self belief, their workshops;
it's easier far to contemplate inner space
when nobody's there in your head. Their fix
on finding themselves can tear up your best beliefs
when even a moderate talent at drumming
connects them to shamanic gods. I'm packing my bags.

Rennie Parker

13

Magpies

Of course it was a whale – that giant skeleton
suspended outside the faculty building.
But as soon as you said *What's that then?*
all the mammals I ever knew sensed my panic
and hurtled en masse out of the unstable ark of my head.

I made an abject stab at it. A mean smile rippled your face.
Don't you wish you'd done a degree in a real subject?
And I think of you categorising, scrutinising. Pinning
dead insects to a board. I can imagine by the age of five
your tide of logic would have drowned out Noah,

your imagination, the hapless raven sent out too early.
I know what ravens are and can identify their cousin crows
the magpies. Today, as I threw open your serviceable curtains
I saw one cawing in a nearby ash. I waited ages
but no others came. You wouldn't understand.

Kathryn Daszkiewicz

14

Snakes

I'm here to listen, he says
and smoothes the space between us.
Unlistening he runs
his polished measure over me,
pumps arms, pivots hands,
rotates wrists, commands eye swivels,
beams at the snake spirals he has me draw.
Better than mine, he lies.

Content, he offers me his arm,
and offers too his malediction:
Things will get worse!
Cleanly he chops through hope
then slivers and slices it dead,
conveys with oiled assurance
how others have imagined improvement
only to be proved wrong
for like a slow-moving escalator
the disease, relentless,
will progress.

I query his catechism of certainty.
His suit grows darker, his smile
wider as it cracks around the mouth.

June Hall

Location, Location

The Attractions Are Closed Today

It is always raining, it is raining again
It is piling down with pluvial generosity
As fast as the devil can spit –
There will never be any politeness about it
Because it is raining to hell and back
Where the houses crowd like unlovely teeth
And the acneous hillside, raw with red estates,
Spreads its developing faultline.
This is indeed Mount Misery as marked on the map –
People are running with bags on their heads
To the dank shops' embrace;
Only the civic statues are brave enough
For this is a town of theatrical disillusion
Where under the sorrowful arms of streetlamps
A thousand hearts are slain.

Rennie Parker

Flotsam

The dirtiest beach in England
makes it hard to love dogs,
drinkers of Coke, scoffers of chips.
It's lunchtime, and the shabby winter sun
shambles across the sky. A wind from Siberia
seeks our bones. We hunch against it.
The shelter we cannot use
makes it hard to love lovers. See the walls,
full of sour slanders – who shagged, who sucks –
the wooden floor is awash with evidence.
On me like tar, sticky and persistent,
the melancholy of the out-of-season
hard-to-love town by the sea.

Ann Alexander

Coldstream Cottage, Ardnamurchan

It's a small white house beside the sea
where the hills are steep and the sky is low
and sheep meander from scree to scree
and sometimes you see a fishing boat go.

The yellow lamplight welcomes you
to a seat by a fire that warms and glows.
An ill wind flusters outside, it's true
but it's calm inside as the darkness grows.

You say, *There's nothing to fear tonight,*
I can rest in peace. If it were so
a haven might mean the world was right.
The floorboards creak and the curtains blow.

Sleep meanders from scree to scree
and the hills are dark and the moon is low.
You hear the snuffling of unease
on the stones, by the door, at the back window.

You toss in a sea of quilted dread
as the black mouth opens, long and slow
and swallows you in your safe white bed
dreaming. You are the last to know.

Helena Nelson

From Room 5

Strange place, Launde,
no cat.
And the starlings have left
Piccadilly Circus, and the magpies
from the Cemetery at Kilburn. They
have all followed me here.

Then there's the howling
which no-one else has heard.
Perhaps an Abbey attracts it.
Perhaps all Abbeys have howling.

On the horizon is a grazing horse
that I happen to know is a clump of trees.
Nearer, a four legged golden creature
stretches up, resting skinny legs
on the tree trunk and rips
the sheltering canopy.

Then there's the car. Who would park
all night long in the middle of nowhere
outside an Abbey gate? Is it
like parking outside a police station?

Then there's the howling.

Berta Freistadt

Heritage

Dustless millstones mark the path
to the museum.
Ploughshares gleam in welcome,
clart and clay a murky memory.
Strange wooden implements
with sweat-smoothed handles
lean indolent against the wall
like teenagers on a Saturday night.
We gaze in awe at butterchurns,
Tilley lamps and washboards.

Then, draped across a chair,
a pair of white cotton drawers –
These belonged
to Mrs Campbell of Boghead.
She stitched them herself.
Notice the fine needlework.
We notice. And notice too
displayed in sepia, Mrs Campbell
long-skirted, high-buttoned,
a proud woman, thankfully unaware.
Remind me, you say, to put it in my will.
'All my knickers to be burned.'

Margaret Wood

Dinner in La Coruña

Old hands at this, we order *percebes, minchas,*
cigales, cabrachos and *lamprejas* – but this
does not please our waiter who insists
we use the English version of the menu
from which he warmly recommends
Scrambles of Tender Garlics, Wide Open
Olives, A Sort of Fish, Weak Rice
with Snips of Lobster, Toast of Turnip Greens
with Hat of St. Simon and Comb of Pork,
A Small Bowl of Rice with Tasty, Tasty Bacon,
and – with a final flourish, he conjures up for us
Today's Specials – Galician Back-of-the-Knee
or Warm Escalabola with Cod's Tears –
in a last bid for independence, we settle
for A Crispy of King Prawns, followed by
Pale Ice-Cream with Saucy Oranges and Scum.

Angela Kirby

The Speech

The voice goes on, a flat, unending drone.
When did he start? Today or yesterday?
Ring, ring, please ring, I urge my mobile phone.

The audience has aged and turned to stone.
A few slip out ('I'm off to the café').
The voice goes on, a flat, unending drone.

A pause. Our hopes are raised! But then a groan –
He carries on. I close my eyes and pray:
Ring, ring, please ring, I urge my mobile phone.

A woman faints: they dab her with Cologne.
She's better off unconscious I should say.
The voice goes on, a flat, unending drone.

Why can't I leave? I've no will of my own.
Some astral force decrees that I must stay.
Ring, ring, please ring, I urge my mobile phone.
The voice goes on, a flat, unending drone.

Connie Bensley

Beached

I lie here, beached, like Gulliver,
tethered to this bed by tubes.
Nearby others lie immobile,
our captors care for us ruthlessly
and we are reduced.
I am, apparently, 'D2: Gall Stone',
'D3: Appendix' lies beside me
morphined into submission
and 'D4: Post Op' is asleep.

Even when they use our names
they are the wrong ones.
They call me 'Mary' and D5 answers
because they have stolen her name and given it to me.
I am no relation to this name on my wristband.
I am no relation to 'Gall Stone'.
I am a poet, the bard of bitterness,
the philosopher who cannot argue away calcium,
the explorer of the lexicon tied down by type.

D4 sails his yacht on pillowy seas
and cries out in his sleep to 'Come about.'
D3 corrals her children to school.
D5 rules her empire with love.
We are people of power,
but our captors do not know this.
Soon we will take our stands, carry our bags,
march out heads high, cast off our wristbands,
reclaim our lives.

Liz Woods

Outpatients

Glum. That's the word. Today's word.
with your current difficulties the letter said.
Now here I am. Ready and waiting.
This waiting room's the same as any other
only smaller and attempting reassurance.
In case you feel tempted to bolt.
All in a day's work, it must be.
No-one else here with current difficulties.
Will he ask, I wonder, how I planned to do it?
Someone's stolen the drawing pin
from the notice about the Samaritans.
It swings to and fro. You have to read it
sideways. If someone comes in they'll think.
But then I am, after all. We all are.
Perhaps they keep us from one another.
Leave fifteen minutes between appointments
so the consultant can write up notes,
have a pee, ring the wife, do press-ups.
I didn't want to be seen. Collar up stuff
like in a gangster movie. No cigarette.
We need a bar but that's no doubt forbidden.

Carole Bromley

Sleepless in Brum

there's an interconnecting door
and I   widowed   on this side
am just sinking gratefully
into the deepest depths
of the comforting arms of sleep
when they clatter in next door
and get straight down to it
treating me to all the sound effects
except words   there are no
words   neither kind nor crude

I'm jagged awake to consider my options

do I   bang on the door
        switch on the telly very loud
        sing She'll Be Coming Round The Mountains
        When She Comes when she comes
        shout would she like me to call the police
        or could they at least try to sound
        as if it's a joyful transaction

        simply scream at the top of my voice
        shut the FUCK up

I churn these choices round the bed
picturing   rejecting the consequences
until suddenly it spasms to an end
they're done and silence billows through
and we can all get some sleep

except I   fuck it   can't

Gina Shaw

Viewing at the National

We have stood a full ten minutes gazing at St. Lucy,
her eyes heavy-lidded on a plate like two sad oysters,

then walk into the next room where the attendant
looks you up and down, then strolls behind us

wanting you under some restraint, on a ribbon
maybe, like Uccello's dragon. Whatever happens

it won't be on his patch. A lecturer glances, stiffens,
parades his tourists to a distance, as if you might

ignite or run amok, as if whatever foreign field
or training camp I found you in had set you ticking.

You are too dark for comfort, too broad, too much
the long-pelted bull, your shoulders boxed to hide

your neck, your walk a swing of supposed
violence under your East End coat, as we pass

between massacres, torture, beheadings,
flayings, tearing by beasts, until in the cold air

we breathe out under the portico. *Not my cup of tea
really*, you say, and lay a finger lightly on my arm.

Marianne Burton

The Poetry Reading

She's all virgin ear and he's good-looking.
He reads: she squeals delight. Her body's rocking
In time to his tongue's rhythms. He, for once,
Is able to discern a sound response.
Her jeans splay out; her hand hangs somewhat near
Her third, instinctive, pulsing nether ear.
The other women in the circle fade
To a mere backdrop. Certainly she's made
His evening. 'Give us more,' she cries
When he folds up and makes as if to rise.
And he obliges; finally withdraws
To her loud *SUPER!* – and some pale applause.

Gerda Mayer

The Party, Let It Be Over

Never, no more, the reluctant fixing of dates,
the ruinous shopping, the endless list
of mates and must-haves; those we dread,
but owe.

Worse still, some other bugger's bash;
the taxi ride through sharp edged neighbourhoods,
arriving late, cleaned out of cash, in a hail
of false hellos, small-talking over sixties songs
and hyper carbohydrate. Cheesy Wotsit smile
bared for the kiss, we launch a dozen conversations.
Michael's broke. Spurs won. Jack's dead.

Chattering towards pie-eyed, we join
the jammed and sandwiched women; groped
by blokes attempting furtive passes, sideways-scrutinised
by wives, found wanting.   All the gatherings
we should by rights have missed
show in our pinched and painted faces.
Semi-pissed,

we wheel out all the tired old jokes,
watch our watches, pocket the borrowed fare,
slip slide to freedom via the loo; then taxi home
to the longed for chair, without our reading glasses.
Never again!

The phone. A party? *Wonderful.* When?

Ann Alexander

Speaking in Tongues

Frisk Draft

What happens to all the no no words,
the *and*s, the *but*s, that *suddenly*?
Do they go to some better place
where there are no rules about what stays in,
where *the* no longer fights with *that*, where all the *ing*s
relax together in no great rush to be immediate
and *pronouns*, no longer dangerous, sit down
and break bread without once getting *personal*
never mind *possessive*, where *abstracts* discuss
the merits of not being particular, of not turning
into wardrobes and pub names, where *tell not show*
is the name of the game and *clichés* are OK
and nobody calls them trite or quibbles
about who said what first and if it matters.
Do *mixed metaphors* congregate in the pub,
stop trying to be something they're not
and even buy a pint for that *old pun*
who's propped the bar up for so long
he's become part of the furniture
and even his *doggerel*'s forgotten the way home?

Carole Bromley

For I will consider my new mobile...

For I will consider my new mobile
For it possesses twenty-seven mysterious functions that my old one did not
For – although I am no slouch – its programming completely defeats me
For the accompanying booklet, though extensive, might as well be written in
Klingon
For it also appears to omit the basic instruction i.e. how to make a call
For therefore I ask my teenage daughter to provide assistance
For this she performs in ten degrees

For firstly she rolls her eyes and sighs dramatically at my incompetence
For secondly she seizes the phone from me, tossing aside the booklet
For thirdly she explains it all v-e-r-y s-l-o-w-l-y
For fourthly she then programs the thing so fast that I cannot follow
For fifthly she hands it over saying *it's ok now*
For sixthly she mutters *sad* when I still need clarification
For seventhly she grabs it back saying *give it here then I'll test it out for you*
For eighthly when she wanders in again I realise she has been chatting to
her friends on it for over an hour
For ninthly when I remonstrate – quite mildly – she shrugs and says
whatever
For tenthly she has now wound me up completely and I am still none the
wiser

For kids today seem to be born understanding these devices
For they seem unable to exist, let alone function, without them
For any passing Martian would think they were a new species, part human,
part Bluetooth

For now I am exasperated with the whole business and chuck the phone
straight into my bag

For when I receive my first call the next morning I discover that
          the ringtone is not the 'Magic Flute' I have requested
For it is 'Dance Wiv Me' by Dizzee Rascal
For an important business meeting is not the best place to find this out...

Liz Crosby

(with acknowledgements to Christopher Smart and his cat, Jeoffrey)

The Fucking Vernacular

'Fuck aye, gie me fower fried eggs fer starters
but fuck sake, mither — *nae fuckin mushrooms.*
An pooer me some tea — hot as fuck.

Pass me the fuckin ketchup, feyther.
Fuck — fuck — it's no cummin oot.
Thick as shit in the neck ay a bottle.

Fuck this looks guid. Fuckin fantastic.
Fuck knows hoo ahm this fuckin hungry —
fuckin *famished.*'

And for over five minutes
he shuts the fuck up.

Helena Nelson

Press 6 to Lose the Will to Live

Thank you for contacting us.
Your call is important to us.
We are always striving to improve.

Calls may be monitored or recorded.
Thank you for holding.
We are currently experiencing high call volumes.

We apologise for this delay.
Please continue to hold.
You are ...thirteenth... in the queue.

We apologise for the hold in answering your call.
Please continue to follow by hash.
If you would like to use our automated delay

please hold your 18-digit customer number
followed by hash.
We are sorry, but that is not a valid hash.

You are now being delayed
to one of our customer service operatives.
They will be able to hold you.

All our calls are recorded to help delay you.
These records are delayed in accordance with the Data Protection Act.
We really do want to speak to you, so please hold us.

We will hold you after this short message:
As part of our ongoing commitment to provide you with excellent
                                        customer holding,
all our calls are recorded and monitored for breathing purposes.

We are currently experiencing high delay volumes.
You are ...forty-second... in the queue.
We will delay your call further at the earliest opportunity.

Please continue to hold us.
We are currently experiencing high holds.
You have delayed at a particularly busy time.

Your delay is important to us.
Please hold us later.

Goodbye

Char March

Out of My Mouth

I've heard all my opinions before
and I'm tired of them.
They fall heavily out of my mouth
and lie around
like tiny, wizened children.

I don't blame you
for stamping on them.
We will do it together
and when the massacre is over
I will begin again –

my thoughts darting and colourful
as tropical birds.
You will hardly know me.
I'll hardly know myself.
So that's a start, anyway.

Connie Bensley

The How-To Manual

Here in the strong medicinal hush of paper
I am looking for a manual on how to do it.

Not Do-It-Yourself. Not Self-Help –
I'd be embarrassed.

No, something strong and subtle,
philosophical even, but not too difficult

and nothing that'll make my shoulder blades
itch when I go to the till.

She's dying and I'm not – or only a little faster
than I was – and up to the oxters

in falling leaves of paper as I am,
I need to know

how not to arrange my face,
to let it be

bare or clouded or whatever is needed
for receiving.

Nobody tells you how to take the sacrament
of sorrow,

the books are strong on how to do,
not be.

So I am going to burn
Mathematics in Easy Stages,

Know Your Own IQ, How To Find/ Keep/
Lose a Relationship,

Meditation for Busy People, The Essential
Buddha/ Jung/ Freud/ Lacan, ...and although

there are sinister precedents for book burning,
this will be a party.

I shall open my mouth vulgarly wide to take,
gamey and wild,

the gift of someone else's sorrow
on my tongue.

Kate Foley

Checklist

Have you a name or distinguishing feature?
Do you suffer from any sensory deception?
Are your eyes male or female?

Have you passed any port/ strait gate/ needle's eye?
Would you describe yourself as insurgent resurgent
deciduous or snowy?

Is this your body? Did you pack it yourself?
Are you to your best knowledge and belief?
Append proof.

M R Peacocke

Nominal Aphasia

Written following a conversation with my daughter about bicycles...

My words are not my servants any more;
They did not answer me when called upon:
I wanted dynamo; they gave me Thermidor

At first I found it funny – *'merde alors!* –
Where did that naughty little thought come from?
My words are not my servants any more!'

I smiled and went on trying; I was sure
The simple hitch could quickly be undone.
I fished for dynamo and landed Thermidor.

I called the thralls who always helped before
But all their old obedience was gone,
My words were not my servants any more.

I felt the terror then, the groping for
The thing that used to make the light come on.
If I need dynamo, what use is Thermidor?

It's like the quiet closing of a door,
The crossing of a private Rubicon.
My words are not my servants any more.
I wanted dynamo; they gave me Thermidor.

Ann Drysdale

Riddle
from the Dictionary of Modern Thought

First ask the question

And make sure it's an
epistemological one

Then you can make
a metaphysical assumption
about an ontological problem
and come up with the answer

(*see also*: epistemology, metaphysics, ontology)

Such is modern thought

If you can think it

full Marx

Joy Howard

The Blue Pill

The 47th message of the day says –
I need the blue pill
to help the red pill to work.
(cornflakes-eggplant-frostbite-wham-bam)
Also, I need the special cream 'Ultra Allure'
to ensure I achieve fantastic erection-48-hour
immeasurable-pleasure-dome fulfilment.
(bing-bong-frigidaire-suncream-turtle-oil)
Apparently, Katya and Ryan and Tanya
are concerned that I achieve my best
and in order to achive an erection of high velocity
                          migrational staying power –
(hornpipe-windpipe-breakdance-kickstart)
and to complete our camping cycle at
an unspeakable terrifying terminal viscosity
(suction-groovy-man-eating-whippersnapper-
muttonchop) I need to take their tablets both
before, during and after.
How did they know we had bought a tent?
And that we were looking forward to the Lakes?
It's so kind of them to care.
It's the 47th message of the day. (heartthrob
-big-gob-Alan Titchmarsh-loose-cob-ambi
dextrous-kettleshank-multimedia-middlemarch.)
I have SUCH high hopes for Windermere.

Helen Burke

Word 2000 Assists with a Poem

Thinks I want to write a letter;
doesn't understand poems, confusing
start of line with start of sentence.
Twitches eyebrows. The poem
wanders across the page finding its shape.
Paperclip is jumping with nerves:
'Do you want help?' I do, but not the kind
computer brains can give me. Yet it may come –

a memory bank of images, a button,
instant poems untouched by human psyche,
drop-down menu for *upbeat, nostalgic, funky*
a list of metres arcane as Book Antiqua
and Times New Roman, click on terza rima
or sonnet to apply the formal settings
to the current selection. Paperclip enquiring
'Do you want to write an epic?' Let me be thankful

all it does now is gesticulate
as the poem spins out of my wrists
leaps from keys to screen, takes a twist
away from its start, doubles back on itself,
ducks under, overlays its own meaning.
Paperclip, dismissed, slinks in dudgeon
out of the weaving page. It knows
I have performed an illegal action

but doesn't close me down. Briefly I savour
the spider's satisfaction at the heart
of perilous creation. The whole web's up
and interlocking to its own pattern,
hoping to lure, frail as a single thread.
Spelling, grammar – I run the standard checks.
But there are words beyond the dictionary,
grammars not easily parsed.

A C Clarke

Thank you for thinking of us

no shards, no lozenges, no litanies
no seagulls, no patinas
no abstract nouns, no adjectives or very few
no haiku

no feelings named, no jokes explained
no smart-arse quips, no rock lyrics
no cats, no dogma

no chopping herbs at kitchen windowsills
no shock tactics, no eating afterbirth
no highbrow quotes, no dream tropes

no obscure myths
no bits in foreign languages
no Shakespeare for the sake of it
no lists like this
no ellipses like these...

no one-word lines, no full rhymes
(unless you're Tony Harrison)
no sing-song rhythms – no *di-dum*
di-dum di-dum, di-dum di-dum

no facile puns, no lies, no libel, no obscenities
no soul-baring
no lambent, incandescent anything
no slips in tone or register

and hey –
no publisher

Julia Deakin

Alien

I am a stranger in a foreign world
don't understand a single sign or symbol.
Meaningless cacophony unfurls,
semaphore of mouth and hand like windmills.
It drowns all study leaving me perplexed,
all language seems a silent coded school
with me a stupid pupil; frowning, vexed.
The Earth spins round according to some rule
with planets pinned and ordered in their course.
Just I am lost, a star beyond control,
a desperate meteorite, no sense but force
that rushes faster than my crying soul.
Let me be still and in that stillness find
translation, silence and a peaceful mind.

Berta Freistadt

Travelling Blight

Delayed

The last time I was here was 1967.
February. Just short of Valentine's Day.
I was crying then too. Huge drips
fell on my red corduroy coat,
smudged my white fur muff.

I'm filling in a complaints form,
estimating my total delay at four hours.
Have you ever tried to kill four hours
at Birmingham New Street?
It's enough to make anyone weep.

Earlier I wandered round the centre
looking for landmarks
but the Rotunda and the Bullring
had gone and Gino's where we shared
an emotional cup of tea.

The 'overall station environment'
is much the same though. I can feel
the shiver of your fingertips
on the back of my wrist
as I tick the 'very dissatisfied' box.

Carole Bromley

Sheffield and Beyond

some of us are reading   some chatting
some watching the tracks

he's taking alternate guzzles
from a large bottle of cider   strong
and a bottle of wine Australian red
both nearly empty now

the drink has warmed up his tongue
and he starts to intone
fuc-ki-nell   fuc-ki-nell
rising to a climax of shout and stamp
to pause and repeat   pause and repeat

some of us wonder if he'll puke
pee his pants   get violent
some worry about the girl next to him

till a new passenger at Sheffield says
you'll have to shift mate
that's my seat   reserved

his brain can't quite wrap round the message
his feet don't quite remember
what   fu-fuc-ksakes   his legs are for
he drops back down   fu-fuc-ksakes
tries to rest his hand on the notice
plastered to the window

so they come for him at Derby
two large dark uniforms but not unkind
the man carrying his gear
the woman holding out her hand
come on sweetie let's get you sorted
taking his hand like a mother
teaching a toddler to walk
come on sweetie   that's right
you can do it   good boy

and he goes like a lamb
and just like that his journey's over
while the rest of us go on
some reading   some chatting
some watching the tracks

Gina Shaw

Auto da fé

One must feel a certain pity for the cones:
under the tarmac stand the skeletons.
The conical red of the penitents' hoods
is all that shows, at the edge of the road,
of heretics in their flame-patterned cloaks
lining the highways in a scarlet snake.

Motorists in their cars and coaches
swear at the immolated wretches;
venting their spleen, they rant and curse
as they crawl in the heat past the long procession
of fugitives from the Inquisition,
deafened by taunting, shouts and jeers.

Ignoring the plight of the damned beneath,
crazed followers of the new true faith
rev their engines in desperation,
thickening the air with foul emissions.
Under the bitumen of car-choked summer
the fires of hell make the heat haze shimmer.

Lyn Moir

My Least Favourite Flight

There are more sensible places
to throw a tantrum than during
turbulence over the Black Sea,
overhead lockers rattling,
all our lives hanging in the balance.
Better places to spill red wine
and command a fast replacement.

First glance back at us in Business
– third estate trash – and the stewards
from Economy come running
in soft leather pumps to restrain
this lush, who was, his neighbours say,
half-cut before ascent. A toddler
stands aghast to see an adult

throw his food into the aisle. While
in the corner by the toilet,
curtained round and meekly silent
a bundle sits in a blanket.
I don't know what it is, but I
have my suspicions, and think
it won't be filing a complaint.

Marianne Burton

Ulan Bator

This last part of the journey has turned into
a pitiless trek to places unknown, the horizon
receding ever farther into the distant dust.
I sailed past Byzantium so long ago
its fabled riches are fading now
even from memory, giving way
to the faceless waste of the solitary steppes,
to long tree-less plains of un-imagination,
in this dead man's watch of the pre-dawn.

I pitch my tent these days in barren fields.
Comfort lessens as my household goods
get too heavy to carry, as bits of myself
get left behind. I am hardly aware of myself
as I put one weary foot in front of another,
walking to who knows where or why.
I suppose there is a destination, but I am forgetting
where it is, and have no hopes of arriving
or of finding it as I expected it to be.
The journey, simply moving on, drives
away all thought, and all desire, and
the wind-howling waste encroaches on all sides.

Rosemary McLeish

The Secret Policeman's Neck Massage

They're taking us in circles. We're the last
load of the year. The quota filled,
the borders close when we depart.
Right from the start the auguries
are bad: the runway shared
with three thin cows, one shepherd,
a bewildered flock of sheep.

The country's beautiful but scarred
with concrete bunkers, the people scared
to speak to us. Tirana's barred
although it's on our destination boards.
So we go round and round.

Pitch dark by three, and vehicles don't use
their lights, what vehicles there are:
twelve army lorries, Chinese-built,
one clapped-out twenties car
are all we've met today.
The potholes knitted up with tar
approximate a road. Tar's easy here,
it grows like daisies. Nodding donkeys pull
out oil from barren landscapes, bubbling
in pools over the soil. The smell of fuel
brings back the queasiness.

We judder on. This ancient bus
has worse suspension than a rusty tractor.
The stench of petrol, raw, is just too much:
I'm face down in a ditch, horizon spinning…
I see the polished boots, suppress a shiver,
security is not a factor now.
Firm hands support my head, their thumbs
rotating, soothing, smoothing with another
rounding motion, circular diversion:
the secret policeman's neck massage,
more tender than a lover's.

Lyn Moir

Dear Rucksack

I cannot understand why you are so heavy.
I cannot understand why you are so leaden.
Today you are shedding baroque tears.
I've done everything I can for you.
I have taken you to several traditional restaurants.
You have eaten pumpkin soup with truffles.
A traditional gypsy has played to you.
You have been fed chocolate cake with sweet almond sauce.
You have loitered in dark doorways in medieval Prague.
You have walked where the Golem walks.
You have seen the oldest bed of the Hapsburgs in Vienna.
You have seen the toilet of Franz Joseph –
the one with the little blue horses on.

You have sat on the birthing chair of the Duchess of Duval
who was buried with her favourite horse.
You have been trampled underfoot on the Viennese Underground.
You have been locked in the Hungarian Parliament due to a chefs' convention.
You have been asked to leave an art-gallery and a Strauss waltz evening
for fear you were a security risk.
You have inadvertently been left on a funicular in Budapest.
But, I came back for you.
So, why so queasy??
Like me, do you yearn for Heathrow –
And the complete lack of mosaics, marble, and chandeliers
in the toilets??

Helen Burke

Air Hotel: Day Room

The rooms mass side by side behind glass fronts,
with tiled floors and walls for easy swabbing down.

Our room smells neutral, not even of cigarettes
or Jeyes. Two tourists, two cases. Nothing unpacked.

The agent arranged it near the airport,
I think we are the only ones here.

There is a restaurant with many tables
and no guests. The waiters are waiting.

There is a guard at the street gate. We're so rich
the beggars and mutilated poor might eat us.

We shower, lie on the bedspread, transparent
under the neon strips, scared of the sheets

– sex is unthinkable, kissing disgusting –
while past transactions settle down about us

and the room hums with commerce, no mouth
rules, torn notes throbbing with shigella.

Something's dirty. But not this room as such.
And we've always obeyed the Rough Guide,

kept Wet Wipes ready at all times and washed
our hands after throwing money about.

Marianne Burton

Miss Pretty

Miss Pretty-as-a-Picture
boards our rush-hour train,
beats two pensioners
to the only free seat
and sits there
glowing.

Miss-Too-Pretty-by-Half
crosses one slim leg
over another, admires
the pale leather of her boots,
her moon-glow nails,
tosses back a swag of hair
and, glancing round
to assess the effect,
bestows a smile
upon the rest of us,
drab strap-hangers all.

Little-Miss-Far-Too-Pretty
For-Her-Own-Good
does not know
that she has spinach
on her teeth.

Angela Kirby

Eurydice on Skye

The walk took six hours and five minutes
what am I saying
the walk took an eternity
you dragged me back from eternity into time

The walk took six hours and five minutes
the book said four and a half hours
but that would be on a fine day
would it not
a fine day after fine days of fine days
with a good springiness underfoot
not a mass of bogs

You were determined to get it done
in four and a half hours

It could only be done
by keeping ahead of me
not stopping to admire sheep
or the darkness of the hills
or the movement of the light

If you keep far enough ahead
you needn't look back
you don't need an explanation
you just keep rushing
scared of eternity
wanting me back in time

I can't keep up with you
I never could
you were the musician
you don't know who I am

I can't keep up with you
but of course I know what's going on
I've been dead
I've been everything

Then you step in a bog
and look back to tell me
you did it for me

And I'm free to return to eternity

While you walk on
with wet mud up your legs
for six hours and five minutes

Margaret Christie

Migrant

My suitcase stayed behind in Moscow.
Unruly to the end, it stowed away and
lurks, scoffing oily caviar, tippling
contraband vodka. Left out at the last
from my carry-on. I imagine it shrouded
in Kremlin shadows, stifling hiccups,
its murky bulk keeping it mafia-safe.

Meanwhile I pace and fret; await its arrival
from Heathrow. Desperate for its release
from customs, from immigration, I fear
the worst: arrests, fines for disorderly
behaviour, for harbouring a stolen
balalaika, for concealing its guilty
face behind a niqab or a veil.

Wendy Klein

Off On 1

I would just like to say
to you who sat beside me
on the H1 bus
which left at 7.55 am
and took one hour ten minutes
to attain its destination,
that I hope you relished
those two bags of
smoky bacon
you devoured for breakfast
half as much as I admired
the expert way you masticated
smacked and crunched your route
through Oakwood, Smalley, Heanor,
Codnor, Leabrooks, Somercotes,
and maybe I should also mention that
I finally decided
after sixty seven minutes
of intense deliberation
that the music from your headphones
would be best entitled 'mad assassins
sharpen up their axe blades',
though 'fingers on the blackboard
with the needle stuck sonata'
would have come in pretty close.
Thank you also for allowing me to find
that I can manage with the best
of British passengers
to look ahead expressionless
while fantasising wildly on you
v e r y   s l o w l y   s t a r v i n g,
while people way above you stuff
their mouths with crisps
and treat you to the bass note line
of angel choirs for a l l   e t e r n i t y.

Cathy Grindrod

Taxi

The man said he hadn't ever,
not ever, he said, put his prices up.

That wasn't the point, not its purpose;
he liked the chat, the company of souls.

Not that most were very witty.
Sick as dogs most of them.

His neighbour had a dog, big black number,
barked all night, hell of a noise, enough to, well.

Those islands, pretty from a distance,
but he'd never been to any of them,

never felt the urge. Bit of a home body.
Sure, it could be boring, back and forth,

same old route. Soothing though.
Do the bands cut into the flesh? he asked.

Then silence, waves sucking the boat's prow,
the sound of the scull twisting in the water.

Marianne Burton

63

Home Sweet Home

Preferring a Sow's Ear to a Silk Purse

Everyone who comes to the house
tells me how beautiful it is, with its
high ceilings, ornate plasterwork,
great sash windows and marble fireplaces –
what noble spaces! what skirting boards!
what original oak doors! How beautiful
you have made it. Yes, but, I say,
and they look at me bemused: this woman,
what will she complain of now?
It's too big, I can't use all this space,
the time of crinolines is gone. The only
cupboards are in the servants' quarters,
and all my lovely things – my bric-à-brac,
the books, the charity shop bargains –
get lost in all this grandeur. I need
a little low cottage, with nooks and
corners and crannies for my stuff.
I need windows I can open with my own
arthritic hands, lightbulbs I can change
without falling off the top of a ladder,
walls I can paint, a door to the garden,
a kitchen I can just about turn around in.
I need a place that's not quite big enough,
cosy with clutter, with no spare room
for uncompleted projects, which,
like the runts of the litter, would
have to take their chances. I need
a place where I can be myself, and
hear myself think, and snuffle and grunt
quietly, in my own ear, my private satisfaction.

Rosemary McLeish

Learning to Like My Slug of Air

This time next year
my sad gift plant which has
small white flies milling
round it will be dead
or it may have turned
into an insect-eating shrub
that smells of sick.
It stands next to the loud
radiator which will probably
be making the same
wailing noise it makes now.
The gas man said it was caused
by a slug of air.
This may be a vacant
mournful thing inside the pipes
calling for its mate.
No unplugging leech
will bleed it into silence.
This time next year
I may have learned
to like it.

Jenny Morris

Excuse My Dust

It undulates in angles, moved by the draught
That fingers its way unbidden under lintels,
Coagulates in corners, forming swathes
Lent substance by random gatherings of fur.
Over time I have become accustomed to it,
Overlook it mostly; aware of it only
In the uncomfortable presence of others.
It is familiar. It grows. It changes.
Each time the front door opens
It scuttles across the room in confusion.
An old friend not quite, as the phrase goes, with us,
Whose soft hands quiver in a fluttery welcome,
Wild eyebrows asking, aghast, *who are you, who are you?*

Ann Drysdale

Butter Side Down

In this house
as you walk on the floor
it crunches
and I'm not talking
crisp clean deep-pile
carpet   I'm talking
cornflakes

In this house
when you open a door
it sticks
think I'm talking
not-quite-dry satinwood
supergloss?   no
I'm talking
chewing gum

In this house
kitchen smells bring you
running
no   I'm not talking
freshly-baked bread rolls or spice cake
I'm talking
burnt toast

In this house   tripping
from room to room means
what it says   yes I am talking
taking a toss over
cardboard packaging
abandoned shoes
old apple cores
dead batteries
empty crisp packets
yogurt cartons
yes   I'm talking
garbage   household
waste

Couldn't you cry ?   but
in this house
when you lay down your head
on the table
and weep   well
watch out
because we are not talking
polished surfaces
laundered place mats
we're talking
jam
in your hair

Joy Howard

Living in Quotations

This place is disintegrating in front of me
I have knocked the cartoned milk off the shelf already
and the white-tagged towel mysteriously lopes
from the rail on which it is placed. Nevertheless
I am assured that this room is not alive
as the blue-covered landlady appears
with a smile as efficient as scissors
cutting through my cloudy grey bewilderment.
Outside, a two-tone ambulance
stripes the air like wallpaper being ripped
and now I am exposed and unfamiliar,
an abject piece of mortality
wearing the look of alarm: '*I am alarmed
in this noisome acoustic bowl*', testing lightly
the brittle springs of a standard-issue mattress.
Lady, wait;
for here the sour milk is dripping onto the carpet
with the look of a saint's tears
don't you think at least it should be cleaned?
Even the green-tinted child in yonder frame
is departing from the scene
proving that plebeian art is not what it was.
I switch on the TV, aware
that I will be biodegradable quite soon –
surely this stuff is not for my entertainment –
lapidary tiles are aimed at me,
truly this room is diseased
for the clock-stroke-digital-radio will not work
and while the rigid lampshade glares straight down
I hear the unmistakeable off-beat thud
as another hapless guest discovers
that he is comic and arbitrary too,
maybe an alien replicant like me,
an ordinary name on his suitcase, fooling us.

Rennie Parker

Spring Offensive

In the hall
the woodlice
assemble
like troops
on a beach
of sand-coloured
carpet.

Not your regular woodlice.
Not a single
dry spy
in a corner.

These
march
full-length.
Move
in battalions.
These
are in training —
SAS woodlice.

We're keeping quiet
about this.
Like scabies or head lice.

       Meanwhile.

Moths are gathering
after manoeuvres.
And bats
are planning
a fly past.

Josie Walsh

Don't Move the Cooker!

This darksome cranny, dogshit brown
With dingy dollops dribbling down,
Where the last of the toast and the rest of the roast
Do lie beyond eye in the heart of the host.

Where there hangs and dangles the mélange among,
Like the grim little ghost of a guinea pig's tongue,
A sharp-shrivelled shaving of Parma ham
O'er the pitchblack puddle that might have been jam.

The curled-up crust and the long-lost cloth
And the paper-thin skin of the boiled-over broth
They lie as they fell and they sleep there yet
In their breath-blown bedding of gossamer net.

Oh, where would the world be, once bereft
Of gunge and of ghastliness? Let them be left.
O let them be left, leave them in peace;
The breadcrumbs, the dead crumbs, the God-given grease.

Ann Drysdale

How the water stains on my ceiling became the map of South America

When the nail-sick roof let rain in
and claimed new territories on the spare room ceiling,

I didn't look when I made up the bed.
But when you pushed me back

quite unexpectedly, I saw the rain's
cartography afresh, as a new continent

bloomed across the woodchip
hot sliver of Chile pointing at Cape Horn.

So I closed my eyes on the dismal English autumn,
let new seas take me to intemperate climes:

Tierra Del Fuego – land of fire.

Kathryn Daszkiewicz

Unhinged

When the cupboard door gave up on its hinges, I rushed
to take it down before it could fall on heads or toes,
my store

of messy habits exposed to the world who visit,
while I pored over the phone book
for a joiner.

On day two
reaching for the coffee, I found it less of a chore
not missing the choreography of opening
and shutting.

By day three,
I was eyeing every other door, wondering
how many more could be
dispensed with.

On day four,
not much happened. I explored the unrestricted view
for hours till I got
bored.

By day five,
boxes were falling off open shelves, tea bags poured onto the floor
in a soft cascade, cornflakes crunched
underfoot

and I missed the suspense
behind each closed
door.

On day six
the joiner arrived with a set of new hinges,
not before time.

Eleanor Livingstone

Anne Is Decisive

That dratted squirrel squanders my goodwill;
wretched pest.
He silently gnaws the new green sprouts
of my young pines,
chewing the tops and littering the soft ground
with spat bits.
Elbow-deep in flour
I build obese dumplings for the Tuesday stew,
observing through the window
a smudgy agitation at the top of a tree
– Goddammit! –
My hands recoil from the bowl
and grab the 12-bore from the corner;
turning, mealy-fisted, I load and fumble,
catch the trigger in the gathers of my apron
and unexpectedly blast a hole
through the kitchen door.

Jenny Morris

Idle Thoughts

One of the great joys
of a well-ordered life
would be
that the littlest one
should go to bed at night
after a bath
and a story
to a made up bed
with clean sheets
and a fluffed-up duvet
for me to later walk
clear across the floor
of the room
and kiss a sleeping face
feeling myself smile serene
and glowing with none of the
pained expression
a piece of Lego trodden
under the instep
induces

Joy Howard

Nice Work

In here I'm trying to write a poem
while out there a man has come
to clean the hall and landing carpet.
Paul Armitage's Home Cleaning Service,
van in drive, is feeding two diameters of hose
in through the windows, one sucks
while the other blows apparently
and *is it OK if I run the hot tap?*

In here I'm trying to write a poem
going back in time two thousand years.
Out there he *no I'm fine love, no,*
no problem starts up the compressor.
In here I'm hewing granite, out there
he squirts detergent on each stair in here
I'm hauling monoliths uphill on logs
out there he *may have to move the piano*
slightly

In here I'm chanting pagan funeral rites
out there I notice two different tones of suck
then intermittent thuds, clicks and bumps
advancing on the door which I get up and close,
properly, wondering how long
the quarrying took. Out there he's *going*
to have to try the bathroom window
in here I – oh, sod it.

Julia Deakin

Poetic Licence

The Muse

Is with me now
but it won't last.

Like that louche, unsuitable man
who appears from nowhere
and liquefies you with a look,
he turned up unannounced.

Soon, embarrassingly soon,
we were at it together,
going like hammer and tongues
while he intruded into every orifice,
planting words I feared might grow
into something monstrous. He wore
me out, making me feel
sick in the pit of my stomach,
yet marvellously alive. Each day
I woke to find him inside me,
and I writhed on the end of the pen,
enjoying the rank smell, the taste and feel of it.

He's still around, just –
but, I know, too soon will come
the morning when he finds
a better hole to go to,
a fresh brain to mess with. And
all the fizzing fireworks of our few
short months together will be over.

Suddenly I'll feel older,
uglier, fatter. I'll forget
to go to the hairdresser.
Remember to feed the cat.

Ann Alexander

Thumbscrew

Poetry bores me.
I think I will become a poet
so I can bore people.

Inflicting boredom's not so far from pain.
I have always been interested in pain.

I had never thought of poetry like this
till now. I am less bored than I was.
I think dinner can wait.

I have written a lovely poem about a thumbscrew.
Let me show you my new metaphor.

Helena Nelson

A Proper Poem

It's time I wrote a poem with nice long lines
to it I'm always chopping sentences in half and cutting
subordinate clauses into pieces very wasteful of paper think how
many trees I'm killing not to mention under-valuing the whale
by saying that small is beautiful so this time I'm
writing a poem that's got exactly ten words in every
line and see if it doesn't bore people to death
which will be a nice change from chopping down trees.

Joy Howard

On being repeatedly told in pubs that poems are about feelings

Feelings?
Do they pull each other out like paper hankies?
Do they sludge together like beans in a tin?
Do they rattle in shells like peanuts?

Can I find them in the cupboard under the stairs
　in the jars in the pantry
　in the blue steel tool-box?

Can you shave a bit off?
Can you weigh them in the balance?

Do they race to be first?
Are they on TV?

Are you sure these are mine?

Pamela Coren

Risk Assessment

Although poets are covered by knowledge of their insanity,
it is vital that you take the utmost care of your poems,
and are seen to be doing so.

Risk Assessment requires poets to ensure the safety
of their creations. We ask you to reconnoitre your inspiration,
to check that you are thoroughly familiar with your route,
and take note of potential risks for readers. Bear in mind
that your audience may be inexperienced in terms of poetic
understanding, and fitness to undertake late night
philosophical discussions, or to wear outrageous clothing,
so extra care is required. This is especially true
of writing workshops. It is difficult to anticipate the size,
or talent, of such groups.

Please look at this list of potential hazards.
If any are present (and remember risk is magnified
by wet ink and coffee stains), tick the appropriate boxes,
and ensure that you inform participants.
Keep the party close together when passing the hazard
to ensure everyone arrives safely.

Hazard   If present in the poem (yes or no)
                          If yes indicate location(s)

Steep or rocky stanza divisions
Slippery rhymes and concepts
Images with steep metaphors
Bewildering sections of symbol
Jagged lines or limp endings
Fields with cattle or horses (risky for romantic poets)
Other (please specify)

In an emergency:
Go to the nearest computer to contact emergency services,
including the Broken-backed Poem Rescue Group.
In case of injury to rhythm or sense, if you do not have
First Aid training, see if anyone in the party does.
At least ensure that the patient is put into Recovery Position,
and urgent action is taken (e.g. rewriting) to insulate the poem,
and provide shelter for the poet from hostile critics.
In the case of minor injuries (e.g. a twisted dactyl),
reach for the nearest thesaurus or writer's guide, from where
a new idea can be summoned – have grammar check facilities
available also. Depending on the severity of the incident, either stay
with the individual and keep working on the injured lines, or leave a
responsible person with them, before continuing on a truncated
version of the poem.

Have a good and safe day!

Pauline Kirk

Playing Dirty

Sleep and poetry are twin sisters.
I've a love/hate relationship with them.
One, cold-eyed and blue-lipped, often
runs from me at bedtime, screaming
when I long for her; the other's a slut
with a pomegranate mouth who
pulls me, succubus, from her sister's
tight embrace at three-thirty
with promises of perfection, of symmetry
and threats of what she'll do, neglect me,
if I don't stop crumpling paper.
They are my see-saw lovers, between
the tossing and turning of the one
and the other's sweet dangerous lies
I can't win; they both play dirty.

Berta Freistadt

You Cannot Be a Poet Unless You Have Met the Moose
on the Road and Worked Out What to Do with It
(For Sally, who is partial to long titles)

Every so often you think you might be a poet.
Might have laid out the twigs of a verse
on the beaten track or the mountain path.
Or, on a very good day, a sonnet in the sunlight, even
under duress, a villanelle in the cloistering evening.

But you know, that real poets always rise from their car
or train seats, or move down bus aisles, where they have been
thinking about nothing, or what they need for tea, when
whatever they are travelling in comes to a sharp halt.
And the headlights (because normally it is in the dark)
pick out that image, there, in a flash, indelible for that moment.
And they have to look at it, unmistakeable
against the blue-black sky.

It will be the Moose.
Either antlered, so that the huge head seems to touch the tree tops.
Or the creature will be swaying in late pregnancy across the clearing.
Either way, there will always be a cliff top or ravine to hand.
And, although there could be a score of other people
on that bus or train, or a fellow passenger in the car,
it is the poet, who needs to know what to do with the Moose
who is blocking the way, and has to be dealt with.

The poet ruminates, but quickly, because this is Moose time.
And people need to feel that, long after the poet has gone quiet
and the Moose too, especially the Moose, there are still matters
about the handling and disposal
that require serious discussion, critical consideration.
And that is not nearly enough, it is only the start of it.
Not everyone will be in agreement
with what the poet has done
with the Moose.
As well as that, not everyone will like the poem.

Josie Walsh

89

Naturepathological

Southernwood rosemary lavender thyme
fennel foxglove flower of lime
marjoram applemint sage and rue
this is what I ask of you

all you herbs from old wives' gardens
(those I miss a thousand pardons)
now I need your timely healing
save me from this awful feeling

I am fighting off the urge
(comfrey borage parsley spurge)
to write a sentimental verse
(lady's smock meadowsweet shepherd's purse)

of hearts and souls and country flowers
autumn mists and April showers
honeysuckle   shady bowers
sundials marking off the hours
morning dew and ivied towers

so lend me please your magic powers

from violets shy and new leaves glossy
branches gnarled and pathways mossy
keep me by your curing graces
and your honest homely faces

stock and wallflower primrose pansy
hollyhock lungwort dog-rose tansy
any time now I'll begin it
help me or I'll put you in it

geranium pennyroyal and guelder
chamomile clove-pink golden elder
chicory sorrel woodruff mace
I feel it coming on apace

pimpernel marigold feverfew
elecampane and heartsease too
horehound bergamot and bay
won't you make it go away

or will it be as I feared
(henbane toadflax old-man's beard)
I shall write myself to sleep
on my overheating compost heap

Joy Howard

(m)

I want not to care who(m) I offend.
Everything I write is filtered through (m).
She gets everywhere, into the lowering
of (my) voice, the knowledge of (my) place,
the keeping of (my) legs together.
I'd like to break out, and burden you
with every last word of my sorry story,
but she says: that's enough now,
mmm?

Rosemary McLeish

Artefact

This poem will
disintegrate
as you read it –
see the words
fade
and fall apart,
see the curator
sweep them
into the
corner
with his
dusty
broom –
lock
the glass case
turn
and leave
the room.

Connie Bensley

How Poets Handle Shit

Shit happens. Everybody gets their share;
the sorry stuff doesn't discriminate –
it hits the fan and then it's everywhere.
Nobody ducks until it's far too late.
A canny lass can never have too many
plans for confronting an emergency.
A sonnet is as good a way as any.
It did for Shagsberg; it'll do for me.
So sock it to me, Sunshine. I can take it.
I'll dredge the sludge for something new to say.
I'll squeeze the mental Plasticine and make it
sing itself. Waste not, want not. That's the way
Creative Writers learn to deal with it.
This is the way a poet handles shit.

Ann Drysdale

Lesstina

She's emptied every bottle, red and white,
and ninety minutes left to meet the dead-
line for the competition of the night:
a verse that isn't rhyme, but pattern-led.
But Parrott indicates that rhyme's all right
and in the glass there's still a drop of red…

Her body thermostat has hit the red,
her skirt's up and her knickers showing white,
but there's no-one around so that's all right.
The spiders and the moths are playing dead.
Her spiral pencil's still got plenty lead.
(She doesn't mind that it's the black of night.)

But inspiration's keeping stumm tonight,
that bible's far too boring to be read;
and she's convinced it should be 'spirit' led –
just not the kind that's scriptured, black on white.
Not all her brain cells have yet joined the dead
and so the moving pencil starts to write.

Dispensing now with her accustomed rite
of calling to her muse (a jaded knight
with jaded horse – it isn't easy being dead),
she numbers out the rhyming lines in red,
a half a dozen squiggles blot the white
and blue-lined page (as snow is lined by sled).

So now the damn thing's rhyme *and* pattern-led,
and *number*-led – surely *that's* not right!
She questions motives, wonders idly why it
seems important to participate tonight
and knows ambition is at fault, that red-
lipped tart that wants to knock 'em dead.

But you, my friends, my peers, are not knocked dead
for you, by truer instincts, have been led.
A hundred years: your poems will still be read
while these weak lines (if justice – right –
prevails) will mulch the bushes in the night
and cower meekly under starry white.

So, pale and ghostly white, but not quite dead
– my insights in the night, the path that led;
a warning stop-light, rightly set to red!

Anne Stewart

E O Parrott: *How to be Well-Versed in Poetry*

95

Phase II. The New Application Form
(Poetic Advice and Assistance Scheme)

PLEASE COMPLETE IN BLACK INK

1. What is the poem's name.
   Is the poem ever known by any other name.

2. Where does the poem reside. Tick one box only.
   a. In your head – *pro non scripto* ...
   b. On a dozen scribbled reverse sides of junk mail letters ....
      somewhere
   c. Last week it was in a box under the bed.
   d. Neatly, in a PC file.

3. Does the poem have any passport benefits.
   (Note: this is not asking if the poem translates well.)

   Tick one box only, no-one likes a smartarse.

   a. A major competition win.
   b. It appeared in The Rialto.
   c. Three times shortlisted for Shit Creek Review.
   d. It's the nation's favourite.

4. Any other benefits or credits.
   a. It's long.
   b. It's short.
   c. Your mum quite likes it, if it's the one about the cat.
   d. It's not a villanelle.

5. Does the poem have any capital – such as capital letters.

6. What, if anything, has the poem earned – or learned – in the last
   seven days.

7. Note: You must have seen evidence of the poem's eligibility.

   What proof have you seen. Tick all boxes applicable.
   a. Unusual imagery.
   b. Imaginative use of language – *mutatis mutandis*
   c. It is not in the first person, or the I is not you.

d. It has invented a new poetic form.
e. It has not invented a new poetic form.
f. The I is not God, or doubtful, or maybe it is.
g. It half rhymes - or half of it rhymes.
h. Repetition, deviation, lyricism, repetition.

You must retain copies of this evidence in your reading.

If you have not seen evidence, why do you think the poem eligible for advice and assistance. Explain *brevitatis causa* in rhyming couplets.

Eleanor Livingstone

Poem

this brick
wall where I bang
my head   after I stop
it exudes such significant
silence

Gina Shaw

All Worked Up

The Copywriter

At the end of a long corridor, in a small room, they sat me down.
Sell this, they said, reverently placing The Thing on my desk.

We want green fields, contented cows, and springtime fragrance.
Give us hand-crafted, full-bodied flavour, satisfaction guaranteed,
in fifty hand-picked words, and do it by Friday lunchtime.
For the Client Cometh.

I stared at The Thing for a long time, there in the dark room,
with one grimy window looking out on the NCP multi-storey car park
where my panda waited among the jaguars.
And on Friday they returned.

The Client has Cometh, they said, *he sits and waits among*
the original Van Goghs in the Italian marble foyer, sipping
the finest French wine. What have you come up with?

I read: *Made from the pickled brains of dead babies,*
and the sludge left over at the sewage farm, processed by robots
and packaged in a tin which costs more than the stuff inside,
to be sold at one hundred times its worth to the undead. Try some.

They stared at me for a long time, there in the dirty cell,
with the broken window looking out on the six lane highway
where no-one but the mighty dare venture.
Brilliant, they chuckled. *We'll sell millions.*

Ann Alexander

Subject: Spring

Hi folks! I want to start
by saying thanks to everyone
involved in Winter's big success.
Well done line-managers and staff
for thinking right outside the box
yet still liaising as a team
strategically to implement
our 'Vision of the Seasons' scheme.

Which brings me, sadly, on to Spring
where once again I must report
substantial inability to change.
This time last year we surely all agreed
that we must rationalise
in order to preserve our target rate
for future growth, and that
unnecessary duplication is a price
we simply can't afford to pay.

Take one example: green.
There's far too many shades
available for what is wanted
which is just to show the
better weather's on the way.
And as for blossom
fine. No-one's denying
what its remit is, but does
there have to be so many kinds?

The same effect can be achieved
and brought in under budget
with some basic pruning
and a long hard look at what
effectively is waste,
a sheer excess, top-down
from sky to ground,
a surplus nowhere justified.
Supply exceeds demand.

We can't compete, and what we need's
a leaner, meaner Spring
to bring us into line
with Winter and the Fall,
perhaps with special emphasis
on why there's so much light,
and if it really ought to silver-top
the fields when we already have
(and how!) the sea.

Well, we can discuss the matter
when the Summer working party
reconvenes, but frankly
if we don't take action now
to stem this tide of overproductivity
then I must warn you that I fear
the worst: our roadmap not ongoing
but reversed!

J A Priestman

Equality

She tidies up the wardrobe of my words
and irons out the creases in my thoughts,
tracing round the contours of my days,
her finger crooked – and just a little taut.

She doesn't let me get away with much,
investigates my make-up on the quiet,
applies a firming corset to my moods
and advocates restraint in mental diet.

I've spent a lifetime in her company,
she shows no sign of tiring of the task;
I'd hesitate to test her loyalty, but
there's one pointed question I would ask:
[to our teamwork I'd deny that I'm resistant]
But is she mine – or am I *her* – assistant?

Alison Orlowska

In Business

Loitering here in a comfort break
my head's filled up, woozy with words.
There's a pond in the hotel garden,
a gravelled water feature from the telly.
Are golden carp accountable? My resources
sit out in a spreadsheet, communications
take routes and all the loops snarl up.
I have that in me which shares
and is competent out of its comfort zone
and that which is not. In my is not
is my breathing, and I think if I dozed off
in a meeting I might drift like weed
to where the carp bludgeon the water,
clanking scales rough as elephants.
I've forgotten how to use a comma
and there's no stopping us now, punch-in-air.
That bird calling, I can't answer its notes,
my system's down, impenetrably down
in loam and aggregate tipped in from trucks.

The fish forever gulping flimsy data –
still can't hear a word they say, can you?
Back in our plastic seats,
sandwich heavy and blood-cold
I want to say just O and O
and seal my mouth on all these
careful closed integrities.
A curious trickling, like a low sluice
tracks me through the minutes,
like something tipping hooks about,
a this-way that-way lack, a tricksy current
lifting some turnscrew worm too soft to gaff.

Pamela Coren

105

Word Association

The Director of Human Resources regarded me
as if I were an interesting species of rat,
then said, apropos of nothing
CHLOROPLAST

Quick as a flash I replied,
understanding the procedure well
DOUGHNUT

She seemed pleased. She offered
ZIMBABWE
and I countered with the admittedly obvious
but perfectly innocuous
SPECTROMETER

But without the slightest warning
she suddenly shouted (the bitch!)
KITCHEN APPLIANCE

I was reduced to sobs – wouldn't you be? –
at the images those words evoked.
Imagine, coming straight out with it
just like that. It was evil, evil. I couldn't speak.

When I calmed down, she said again
KITCHEN APPLIANCE as if repetition
would somehow make the words acceptable.

I saw, through my tears,
that my enemy sat behind that desk.
I whispered: keep your rotten job,
if that's the way your mind works.

Ann Alexander

Dramatis Personae: Seminar I

This oblong of print, neatly columnar
does not square with the rough circle
of faces perching here, alert
with expectation or anxiety.
Aaronovitch, George, has not arrived
– he will burst in, furious-haired
three weeks later, having missed
the first act (Explication).
Cahoun, Chris, scarlet with acne
will have left by then for Management
and Business Studies (Resolution).
The list is corrupt, a Bad Quarto –
mis-spelling Lascelles, omitting Ormeroyd –
and will need annotations later:
Tilling, Charlotte, who will sob
behind her long hair in Week Five
(Catastrophe) doesn't know
this autumn is chosen by her parents
for their separation. Jobson,
Greg, will miss class after class,
heedless of warnings. And Beckett,
Samantha, is permanently off-stage
waiting for a cue. We may as well
begin without her.

Christine Webb

And the Echo Won't Tell You a Lie

no-one
who is responsible for literally millions of jobs
millions
can possibly condone the government's tax
on petrol
no-one
could be more sensitive
sensitive
to the threat of climate change
change than we are
we ARE
we've even replaced our rest-room roller towels
with recyclable paper
paper – YES
and before you ask of course it comes from sustainable forests
sustainable of course
of COURSE not in the executive rest-room – *incentives*
there have to be incentives
there are limits....
limits to growth you say?
very unsound thesis that
paranoid in the extreme
extreme climate you say?
say
where?
a few polar bears?
bear with me while I show you our strategic growth chart
chart I said not heart
a bit windy today isn't it
isn't it? ...
papers all over the place...*bear* with me...*where?*
on the 28th floor? don't be ridiculous... it wouldn't fit in the lift
would it?
would it??????

Kate Foley

Sloth for Beginners – Lesson 1

Forget the usual multi-tasking many-hattedness
that keeps you in a spin. You're here to learn
the trick of slothfulness – our time is limited –
so, psyche yourself, start worrying and hurrying
to pump up your adrenalin and – on your marks?
– then we'll begin.

Quickly now! – start slowing down
your metabolic rate. It <u>must</u> be low!
You have your tree? Then up! Up and out
along that branch and get out on that limb!
Now: Slow. Slow. Sloth. Sloth. Slow.
And blink. And rest.

That's it, well done, you've got the hang of it!
(Yes, yes, the people stare in admiration from below.
Well, no need to make a song and dance of it.)
Prepare for shutting down. Shut down in 3… 2…
ah. Next time we'll cover shutting down
without the letting go.

Anne Stewart

Message

Sometimes I visit that website with your picture on
just to reassure myself you're still in the world.
What was it Hannibal Lecter said? *The world*
is a much more interesting place with you in it.
How soberly you're dressed these days
and how tightly you've knotted that tie.

Sometimes I reach out and touch the scar
on your eyebrow where you walked into the shelf
or scroll down to study your colleagues' faces,
wonder which one you might be in love with,
which one annoys the hell out of you,
which one you hate so much you've wiped her hard drive.

Carole Bromley

The Tomb of the Unknown Worker

No eternal flame flickers for me –
I lived by the rules and the clock. A nine-to-fiver,
till I clocked in for my P45.

No gold watch reminds my grey shade
of the empty years emptying the bins.
No blue plaque bears the legend
Here's where she fiddled her life away
along with her expenses.

No-one has put a seat on the park
as a pat on the back for the litter I picked.
Tesco has not endowed
a scholarship in my name,
though I sat at that till
through nine different managers.

I was at the blunt edge.
I took my eye off the ball.
I was surplus to requirements.
I ran it up the flagpole, and no-one saluted.
I hit my head on the glass ceiling.
I suffered from
repetitive strain strain strain.
I passed away after being passed over.

When I handed in my notice,
no-one noticed.

After I died of boredom, I buried myself here,
among the roses. No-one, so far,
has come to pay their respects.
Do drop by. There's room for us all,
here at Dunslavin,
with its quite nice view of the sea.

Ann Alexander

This Is Just to Say

I have kept you
on hold
for fifteen
minutes

and you
are probably
really
pissed off.

Forgive me.
Your call is
important – but
so are coffee breaks.

Eleanor Livingstone

Letter of Resignation

Dear Sir

Stuff your

recycling bins, map-pins, win-wins, acronyms, your post-tray,
in-tray, out-tray, up-yours tray, your 2-finger kit kats, mouse mat
(sit on that).

Keep your

four-wheel drive, A drive, C drive, sex-drive, shared disks, compact
disks, floppy disks, flaccid disks, minicom, CD Rom, dot com, monk
on, www dot, bald spot, brain (not).

Buy your own

duplex, offrex, tippex, semtex, screenkleen, caffeine, windolene,
guillotine, flora lite, megabyte, load a shite web site.

I'm out of here, no fear, fifth gear, way clear.

Enjoy your

hair dyed, bit on the side, hotel guide, quick ride.

When I said I had saved all your records

I lied.

Cathy Grindrod

Great Escapes

The Music Came Through

The big smoothie man
With the big smoothie hi-fi
Wanting to use its power
Over you and me together
(Harmless, you know, with two of them there)
When I wanted to be with you

The big smoothie man
Said Beethoven was better on good equipment
But to me the music came through
On the school's machine,
Scratches and all, in the dining hall,
When the teacher left me alone with you.
Perhaps she knew.

And the music came through
In the practice cells, in the gaps between classes,
The cracks of time, the strain of score-reading
Lightened by playing together –
Symphonies could be duets, duets symphonic.

The big smoothie man
Trying for heroics with fancy machines
Can have the funeral march;
We'll take off with the false return
And the scherzo.
We'll have a trio with our music teacher –
Eroica – the feminine ending.

Margaret Christie

The Back End of a Pantomime Horse

It's a start, said my mum.
Ought the girl? cautioned Gran,
alert to the dangers of running about
with my head on a man's backside.
Trust you to be different, fretted my friend,
who'd like to be Kylie, or Catherine Zeta Jones.

All I could hear was the crowd,
all I could smell was the bum in front.
All I could see was the dirty stage,
his look that said
I am the horse, you are the horse's arse.

It rankled – I grew restless. Tried a few
impulsive kicks. Crossed my legs
at the ankles. Did a pirouette,
held my tail out, straight as a flag.
The crowd adored it, roared their delight.

Then I thought, why not try for
the real thing? I studied the horse,
waiting for Curtain Up. Gave her a name,
lived on water and grass. My legs
grew fur. I kicked off ersatz hooves,
stripped bare. Dreamed myself out
on the plain, blonde mane streaming,
or dripping like willow, down to the
clear pool. I longed to feel
green in my throat, never a soul
astride my back, never a heel
in my heaving side, never a stick
nor a bit nor the pull of a rein.
The front end put his hoof down. Said
It's the not knowing.

Front legs going one way, back the other.
He played the horse in the old manner,
flower behind one ear, hat on his head.
The rest you can guess. One of us had to go.
At pantomime time, I wander the moor
and think of him, knowing that over the rise
my lost herd roams, lifting their heads as one,
calling me home.

Ann Alexander

In Transit

Suspended between departure lounge
and destination,
balanced like a coffee cup
upon the rim of unreality,
stripped of definition,
checked in, checked over, x-rayed,
denuded of responsibility:
duty free.

Lyn Moir

Working Girl Dreams

Today I am called to account
for my profligate use of
recycled cream wove
and digital pens with
Bluetooth transmission
by a dusty minion with
cobwebbed scalp and
incipient ulcer who
stares at my thighs as
he labours his point.

But this evening at dusk
I shall wrap myself
in watered silk and
slide through the tamarisk
to answer the call
to a count whose skin
smells of cinnamon,
whose eyes sweep
the balance sheet of
my soul and uncover
no single deficit.

Alison Orlowska

Bewley's Blues

'Anything else for you, sir?' the waitress said
neat in her lilac uniform:
she took me for a little old man
I know she did –
me, stooped over the table with my poet's notebook,
seen from the back in my smoky-blue trousers
and ice-blue shirt, my hair too fine
worn short that summer.
But I turned my head
and she saw my hyacinth eye-shadow;
my turquoise earrings, caught in the sun,
shed coins of light around the café.
She gave me a horrified look
and a blackcurrant drink.
The look said, 'I haven't done one thing right today!'
and she heard my first-soprano voice (pale blue)
ask for the bill.
Then we were whirling,
the waitress and the little old man,
swirling and twirling,
dancing high
over the bluebell sea.

The pressing crowd in Grafton Street
thought it an advert for Bewley's.

Thelma Laycock

Far Side

The way how, when you go up in a plane, unsettled
by the rush to take off, jostled by mere air and by
how deftly, finally earth has been swiped from you –

how when you've come to terms with this and with being
thrust like miners in a cage through crops of vapour
credible enough for you to want to dodge them

you emerge, into that brilliant blue realm, blinking
like shorn sheep at some apprehended loss but also
simultaneously at such dazzling weightlessness,

and at how heavenly life's old grey clouds look
there below, turned inside out, snow-soft, sun-bright
and level as a causeway you could walk for ever.

Julia Deakin

Early Mass 1944

Et introibo ad altare Dei ... *I will go*
unto the altar of God ... our rusting bicycles
slumped against the railings, we bend our heads
over pews of yellowing pine (that acrid hint of resin),
the cold from flagstones seeps into our knees.

ad Deum, qui laetificat juventutem meum ...
to God, who gives joy to my youth ... mud is frozen
to our shoes, we blow on chilblained hands, the iced
and incense-laden air knifes into our lungs
as we breathe it in through aching nostrils.

Quam dilecta, tabernacula tua ... *how beautiful*
are thy tabernacles ... someone has jammed
chrysanthemums and ivy into a tarnished vase,
the utility candles snap and stutter, weep grey tears
on the altar-cloth, windows gape, their stained glass gone.

Vere dignum et justum est ... *it is truly meet and just* ...
and it seems right to be so hungry and so cold,
as we offer Mass for those at war, our stranger-fathers,
our round-eyed brothers and sisters, gawky
in caps and uniforms too big, too stiff for them.

Ite, missa est ... *Go, the Mass is finished* ...
we throw missals and mantillas into battered baskets,
bike home to breakfast, standing on the pedals,
as we weave between potholes, the wind behind us,
laughing, shouting insults, and suddenly happy.

Angela Kirby

It's All Wrong With Me

It's the wrong time and the wrong pill,
though this pill works wonders – it's a strong pill.
It's not my pill, but such a lovely pill
that it's all right with me.

It's from the wrong box in the wrong drawer
but it slips down so easy I might take one more.
It's not my pill, but perhaps another pill
will be all right with me.

You can't know how happy I am that I found
a whole boxful hidden away.
I won't have regrets 'cos I won't be around,
best forget me is all I can say.

I'm in the wrong game, I've paid the wrong bills,
though these pills are tempting they're the wrong pills.
They're not my pills, but oh such tempting pills
that they're all right with me.

They're the wrong pills in the wrong box.
Though the box is empty it's not my box.
No, what's my box is a wooden box
and that's all right, it's all right,
oh

it's

all

right

with

me

Rosemary McLeish

Imprisoned

The woman is trapped
in a poem
held fast by bars of words
blocked by regular metres.

She suffers internal rhymes
endures assonance
and strange images
has problems with syntax.

She's stuck in a stanza
hammered by figures of speech
major metaphors, similes
edged in by personification.

She's straightjacketed
by sonnets and ballads
is maddened by repetitive rondels
villanelles and sestinas.

She's tortured by stresses
until sensing the rhythm
of her heartbeat
and hearing her own voice

the woman escapes
from all constrictions
and is released
into free verse.

Jenny Morris

On the Train

Unwilling witness to the general fray
of ring-ting jingles, love yous, business deals
apologies and ETAs, I slump
exhausted, tumult-battered,
helpless drifter in a sea of dross.

But surely, love can be defined this way:
as having one to whom it matters
whether you're a speck of dust that whirls
through an indifferent universe
or on the 18.20 from King's Cross.

Joy Howard

Caithness

And now Heather with the weather.

Sun will shine from dawn to dusk.
Skies will be blue as a film star's eyes,
clouds as light as whipped meringue.
Breezes will sway like the hips
of a hula-hula dancer.
A fine day for everyone,
except in the Far North.

There, steel skies laden with stormy boulders
will bear down like a weighted yoke
upon the land. Winds will blow
like the wrath of an ancient god,
like a birthing pang,
like a punch in the gut that bows you down
to shoulder the plough,
to heave the nets,
to wrest the peat,
to hew the grim grey stone
that shapes the life of Caithness.

And then like a blessing evening will come,
a ribbon of peace at the end of the day
stretching long and long and light
till dusk meets dawn.
A gift from an ancient god, perhaps
and only in the North.

Margaret Wood

Market Town

Bus shelter in December. Slate-dark cloud
seems to descend as chilling air attacks
ears, noses, hands. Sullen, heads bowed,
we watch. Two hoodies, booted, their rucksacks
slung on left shoulders jump the silent queue.
An impasse. We sit as they lurk outside.
They will break something: bottles, a taboo.
Our preconceptions must be satisfied.
One lifts his arm, his finger writes in frost
on flimsy glass that keeps us from the wind.
Unknown obscenities. We'll pay the cost
of all graffiti, ignorant, thick-skinned.
       This one will melt and we won't read again
       his 'Merry Christmas' on a dirty pane.

Barbara Daniels

Naming

One airport much like another,
the same eternal corridors,
the same departure lounges.

We taxi to the runway:
below I see white clover in the grass,
a bee, a clump of yellow bedstraw,
a small brown butterfly.

At once the airport turns into
a place where species are defined
by difference. I want to be out there,
on my hands and knees,
naming things.

Gill McEvoy

Finale

Witness

To witness miracles you don't need
to be chosen   remarkable   possessed of gifts
not even lucky over time and place   just
to be alive to what's there fizzing
like fish in a coral garden
brilliant exchanges among souls and worlds

Rub habit from your eye   you'll catch
astonishments such as rascally Jacob dreamed
angelic fooling   starry tricks
on a builder's ladder propped against heaven

M R Peacocke

The Poets

Ann Alexander lives in Cornwall. Her two collections from Peterloo Poets are *Facing Demons* (2002) and *Nasty, British & Short* (2007). Her third collection, *Too Close*, was published by Ward Wood in 2010. Prizes include Mslexia (2007), Bedford Open (2007), The Frogmore Prize (2000) and BBC Poem for Britain (3rd).

Connie Bensley lives in London and the most recent of her six poetry collections is *Private Pleasures* (Bloodaxe Books 2007). She was a prizewinner in the Tate Gallery and Observer competitions and was on the judging panel for the Forward Prize in 2004.

Carole Bromley has published two pamphlets with Smith/Doorstop, *Unscheduled Halt* (2005) and *Skylight* (2009). She lives in York where she teaches creative writing for York University's Centre for Lifelong Learning.

Helen Burke has been writing poetry for 35 years. She has won many national competitions and is widely published in magazines and anthologies; a short film was made of one poem and another poem was set to music. Two new collections are due out this year, as is a children's book which she has illustrated. She is mentored by BBC to write for radio.

Marianne Burton is widely published in the UK, US and South Africa, in places such as *Agenda, Borderlands: Texas Poetry Review, New Contrast, Poetry Ireland Review, Poetry London, Poetry Wales, TLS*, and on Poetry Daily. Her pamphlet *The Devil's Cut* was a PBS pamphlet choice, and her first collection is forthcoming from Seren.

Margaret Christie lives in Edinburgh. Her pamphlet *The Oboist's Bedside Book* (Happen*Stance*) was shortlisted for the Callum Macdonald Memorial Award. She is a member of Pomegranate Women's Writing Group, and makes her living indexing, editing and proofreading other people's words. She also plays the keyboard in a ceilidh band.

A C Clarke has published *The Gallery on the Left* (Akros Press 2003), *Breathing Each Other In* (Blinking Eye 2005), and *Messages of Change* (Oversteps 2008). She is currently working on a poetry collection on the atheist priest Jean Meslier and a poetry pamphlet inspired by the Anatomy Museum in Glasgow.

Pamela Coren is a former teacher of literature at the University of Leicester. As well as academic works she has published poems in many magazines and has one collection out, *The Blackbird Inspector* from Laurel Books.

Liz Crosby has lived in Norfolk for six years. She has worked as a park warden, CAB worker and reference librarian and currently as a volunteer in a charity shop. She gets her main inspiration from people-watching and walking on the beach. She likes frogs, the autumn, pottering around at boot fairs, and creating order out of chaos, and is an Arsenal supporter.

Barbara Daniels has had six collections of poetry published, the most recent being *The Cartographer Sleeps* (Shoestring Press).

Kathryn Daszkiewicz was awarded a writer's bursary by East Midlands Arts in 2001. A selection of her work appeared in the Shoestring Press anthology *New Writing* that same year. *In the Dangerous Cloakroom*, her first collection, was published by Shoestring Press in October 2006 and she is currently compiling her second.

Julia Deakin was born in Nuneaton and worked her way north via the Potteries, Manchester and York to Huddersfield. She won the 2006 Northern Exposure Prize and was a 2007 Poetry Business Competition winner with *The Half-Mile-High Club*. Her first full-length collection, *Without a Dog*, was published in 2008.

Ann Drysdale was born near Manchester, raised in London, married in Birmingham, ran a smallholding and brought up three children on the North York Moors and now lives in South Wales. She has five volumes of poetry in print; four from Peterloo Poets and a fifth, *Quaintness and Other Offences*, from Cinnamon Press.

Kate Foley was a midwife, then changed horses and became Head of English Heritage's Ancient Monuments Laboratory. She now lives in Amsterdam, where she is a poetry editor for *Versal*. She leads workshops and gives frequent readings in the UK, Holland and elsewhere. Her fourth collection is *The Silver Rembrandt* (Shoestring Press 2008).

Berta Freistadt, a prolific and popular poet, short story writer, novelist and playwright, sadly died in 2009. Everyone who knew her misses her vibrancy, her wit, her generosity of spirit. Her enormous courage in enduring a long series of illnesses with her indomitable humour intact remains a source of inspiration.

Cathy Grindrod's latest poetry collection is *The Sky, Head On* (Shoestring 2009). She is the former Derbyshire Poet Laureate and is also a playwright and librettist. She works as a freelance literature consultant, tutor and mentor, and enjoys writing poems of revenge.

June Hall, former publishing editor and literary agent, lives in Bath with her husband and, when they are home, her two student children. She wrote for women's magazines before turning to poetry and has published two collections with the Belgrave Press: *The Now of Snow* (2004) and *Bowing to Winter* (2010).

Joy Howard lives in West Yorkshire. Poetry has always been part of her life, and after retirement she returned to writing, and founded Grey Hen Press. This is her fourth anthology, and she is by no means ready to give up yet. Her second collection, *Refurbishment* (Ward Wood) is due out in April 2011.

Angela Kirby, Lancashire born, now lives in London. Her widely published poems have won several prizes and are translated into Romanian. Her two collections, *Mr. Irresistible*, 2005, and *Dirty Work*, 2008, are both from Shoestring Press. A third collection is due from them in 2012.

Pauline Kirk is the author of two novels, *Waters of Time* and *The Keepers,* and ten collections of poetry. A third novel, *Foul Play*, is due out in 2011. Her poems, stories and articles have appeared in many journals, and been broadcast on local radio. She lives in York.

Wendy Klein has won many prizes in the poetry world and is widely published in magazines and anthologies. Her first collection, *Cuba in the Blood*, came out in 2009 with Cinnamon Press, and a second collection is due out in early 2013. She reads regularly in and around Reading and London.

Thelma Laycock lives in Leeds. Her work has been published in various magazines and anthologies and has been translated into

Hebrew, Italian and Romanian. Some poems have been broadcast on Romania Cultural Radio. She has had three pamphlets published and a new collection, *A Persistence of Colour* (Indigo Dreams Publishing), is due out this year.

Eleanor Livingstone lives in Fife. Since 2005 she has been a Director of StAnza, Scotland's International Poetry Festival which takes place annually in St Andrews. Her first full collection, *Even the Sea* (Red Squirrel Press), was shortlisted for the London New Poetry award in 2010.

Gill McEvoy runs several regular poetry events in Chester (Zest!, The Poem Shed, Poem Catchers). Pamphlets *Uncertain Days* and *A Sampler* (Happen*Stance* Press 2006, 2008*)*. Full collection *The Plucking Shed* (Cinnamon Press 2010).

Rosemary McLeish was born in 1945. After a varied and unsatisfying career through jobs and higher education, she started to paint and write at the age of forty. She has produced two pamphlets and had poems published in magazines and anthologies, as well as exhibiting them alongside art works.

Char March is a multi-award-winning poet, playwright and fiction writer. Her credits include: four poetry collections, six BBC Radio 4 plays, seven stage plays and numerous short stories. She is a highly-experienced tutor in creative writing, grew up in Central Scotland and now lives in the Yorkshire Pennines.

Gerda Mayer was born in Czechoslovakia and came to England aged eleven. Collections from Chatto & Windus, Oxford University Press, Peterloo Poets, Iron Press etc. Her *Monkey on the Analyst's Couch* (Ceolfrith Press) was a Poetry Book Society recommendation. Her *Prague Winter* (autobiographical prose vignettes) was published by Hearing Eye.

Lyn Moir lives in St Andrews. Her second full collection, *Velázquez's Riddle*, will be published in March 2011.

Jenny Morris was born in North Yorkshire and is known as *Ripon Steel*. She writes poems and fiction. Her writing has won awards and been published in many magazines and anthologies. Her latest poetry collection is *Lunatic Moon* (Gatehouse Press). She lives in Norfolk.

Helena Nelson is founder editor of Happen*Stance* Press which specialises in poetry pamphlets. She is also a poet in her own right. Her most recent collection is *Plot and Counter-Plot*, Shoestring Press 2011.

Alison Orlowska was appointed Hampshire Poet for the National Year of Reading, 2008. She has led poetry workshops in schools and many venues. Now living in West Yorkshire she continues to write and works to promote poetry in health care. Two poetry pamphlets: *Roosting with Liver Birds* (2008) and *Reeling in the Dream* (2009).

Rennie Parker was born in Leeds, and now lives in Lincolnshire. She has published with Flambard and Shoestring (next is *Borderville*, Shoestring 2011) and she appears in *The Iron Book of New Humorous Verse* (Iron Press 2010). Her word-based linocuts featured in an exhibition at The Collection, Lincoln, 2011.

Meg Peacocke has been at various times wife, mother, grandmother, teacher, counsellor and small farmer. She has an abiding passion for walking off the beaten track and for music and the visual arts. Peterloo Poets published four collections of her poems between 1998 and 2008. In 2005 she received a Cholmondeley Award. A new collection is due out from Shoestring Press.

Judith Priestman was born in 1951 and grew up in rural Oxfordshire, where she still lives and works.

Gina Shaw lives in Ilkley. She has had poems published in various magazines and in other Grey Hen Publications. She travels on trains a lot where she often meets strange people. She thinks she might be one of them.

Ruth Smith used to teach English but now spends her time travelling and writing poems. Poems have appeared in several poetry magazines, most recently *Magma* and *Orbis*; two forthcoming in *The Interpreter's House*. Other work has appeared in anthologies including *Entering The Tapestry* produced by The Poetry School.

Anne Stewart is founder of the poet-showcase site, www.poetrypf.co.uk, featuring over 250 poets and their work. She has an MA(Dist) in Creative Writing from Sheffield Hallam University and won the Bridport Prize in 2008. Her first collection, *The Janus Hour*, was published by Oversteps Books (www.overstepsbooks.com) in July 2010.

Isobel Thrilling was born in Suffolk, raised in Yorkshire, read English at Hull, worked as Head of ESL in London. She has a son, a daughter and two granddaughters. A prizewinner (Bridport and York), she has been widely published: magazines, anthologies, radio and television. Her latest book is *The Language Creatures* (Shearsman 2007).

Josie Walsh lives in Wakefield where she edits *Under Glass*, a community poetry magazine, at Pugneys Country Park. After retirement and completion of an MA, as well as work in anthologies and magazines, she has two collections published: *Breathing Space* (2004) and *Another Breath* (2009). She is working on *Breathing Still*.

Christine Webb's collection *After Babel* was published in 2004 by Peterloo Poets. Her collection *Catching Your Breath* will be published by Cinnamon Press in 2011.

Margaret Wood grew up in rural north-east Scotland and studied French and English at Aberdeen University. She now lives in Wick, where she escaped teaching to become the local registrar. She's had fiction for adults and children published in mainstream women's magazines. A college course has rekindled her interest in writing poetry.

Liz Woods was born in East Yorkshire and as a child her father read her Tennyson rather than nursery rhymes. She trained as a solicitor but soon escaped to a career teaching law. Liz lives in Cornwall where she working on her first collection of poems, *Hanging Round the Inkwell*.

Index of Poets

Acknowledgements

ANN ALEXANDER 'The Copywriter', 'The Muse' and 'Word Association' *Facing Demons* (Peterloo Poets 2002); 'The Back End of a Pantomime Horse' *Nasty, British & Short* (Peterloo Poets 2007); 'The Party, Let It Be Over' *Too Close* (Ward Wood 2010). CONNIE BENSLEY 'Out of My Mouth', 'The Speech' and 'Artefact' *Private Pleasures* (Bloodaxe 2007). CAROLE BROMLEY 'Frisk Draft' published in *Magma*; 'Outpatients', 'Delayed' and 'Message' published in *Seam*. HELEN BURKE 'Dear Rucksack' *Zuzu's Petals* (Poetry Monthly Press 2007). MARIANNE BURTON 'Air Hotel: Day Room' and 'Viewing at the National' *The Devil's Cut* (Smiths Knoll 2007). MARGARET CHRISTIE 'The Music Came Through' *The Oboist's Bedside Book* (HappenStance 2007). A C CLARKE 'Word 2000...' published in *Poetry Scotland*. PAMELA COREN 'In Business' published in *Iota*. LIZ CROSBY 'For I will consider my new mobile' published in *The Frogmore Papers*. KATHRYN DASZKIEWICZ 'Magpies' *In the Dangerous Cloakroom* (Shoestring Press 2006). JULIA DEAKIN 'Nice Work', 'Thank you for thinking of us' and 'Far Side' *Without a Dog* (Graft Poetry 2008). ANN DRYSDALE 'How Poets Handle Shit' *Backwork* (Peterloo Poets 2002); 'Don't Move the Cooker!' and 'Nominal Aphasia' from *Between Dryden and Duffy* (Peterloo Poets 2005); 'Excuse My Dust' *Quaintness and Other Offences* (Cinnamon Press 2009). BERTA FREISTADT 'From Room 5' published in *The Launde Bag* (Second Light Network 2009). CATHY GRINDROD 'Letter of Resignation' and 'What the Harassed Woman Wished She'd Replied...' *Fighting Talk* (Headland 2005); 'Off On 1' *Laureate Lines* (Derbys CC 2007). JUNE HALL 'Snakes' *The Now of Snow* (Belgrave Press 2004). JOY HOWARD 'Butter Side Down' and 'Riddle' *Second Bite* (Grey Hen Press 2007); 'Idle Thoughts' *Poems While You Wait* (St James's Hospital, Leeds 2008); 'On the Train' and 'Naturepathological' *Refurbishment* (Ward Wood 2011). ANGELA KIRBY 'Dinner in La Coruña', 'Early Mass 1944' and 'Happy Hour at the Pig and Polecat' *Dirty Work* (Shoestring Press 2008); 'Miss Pretty' published in *Magma*. PAULINE KIRK 'Risk Assessment' *Envying the Wild* (Fighting Cock Press 2008). THELMA LAYCOCK 'Bewley's Blues' published in *Airings*. GILL McEVOY 'Naming' *The Plucking Shed* (Cinnamon Press 2010). ROSEMARY McLEISH 'Preferring a Sow's Ear to a Silk Purse', 'Ulan Bator' and '(m)' *How Do You Think the Ladies Ride?* (Bumblebee Press 2008). LYN MOIR 'The Secret Policeman's Neck Massage' and 'Auto da fé' *Breaker's Yard* (Arrowhead 2003). JENNY MORRIS 'Anne Is Decisive' *Urban Space* (NPF 1991); 'Learning to Like My Slug of Air' *Lunatic Moon* (Gatehouse Press 2006). HELENA NELSON 'Coldstream Cottage, Ardnamurchan' *Starlight on Water* (Rialto 2003); 'Blind Date' and 'The Fucking Vernacular' *Unsuitable Poems* (HappenStance 2005). RENNIE PARKER 'The Attractions Are Closed Today' published in *Leviathan*; 'Living in Quotations' published in *Critical Survey*. M R PEACOCKE 'Firing Day' *Speaking of the Dead* (Peterloo 2003); 'Checklist' and 'Witness' *In Praise of Aunts* (Peterloo 2008). ANNE STEWART 'Lesstina' published in *The Launde Bag* (Second Light Network 2009). JOSIE WALSH 'You Cannot Be a Poet Unless You Have Met the Moose on the Road and Worked Out What to Do with It' *Another Breath* (Ox-Eye Press 2009). CHRISTINE WEBB 'Dramatis Personae: Seminar I' *After Babel* (Peterloo Poets 2004). MARGARET WOOD 'Caithness' published as 'Except in the North' in *Making Things* (North Highland College 2009).

Joy Howard is the founder of Grey Hen Press, which specialises in publishing the work of older women poets. Her poems have featured in several anthologies: *Beautiful Barbarians* (Onlywomen 1986), *Dancing the Tightrope* (Women's Press 1987), *Naming the Waves* (Virago 1988), *Not for the Academy* (Onlywomen 1999), *The Argent Moon* (Pembrokeshire Press 2007), and *The Listening Shell* (Headland Press 2010). She is a contributor to Grey Hen's first publication *Second Bite*, also the name of a group of three older women poets who give readings together. She has edited three previous Grey Hen Press anthologies, and published a collection of her own poems *Exit Moonshine* (Grey Hen 2009) about her 'coming out' experiences in the 1980s. She was a Chapter One Promotions Open Poetry prizewinner in 2007, and has been published in ARTEMIS*poetry*, *Sofia*, *Sphinx*, *Lavender Review* and *The Frogmore Papers*. Her poems can be found online at *Guardian Unlimited* and *poetry p f*, and feature in *'Poems While You Wait'* at St James's Hospital in Leeds. A new collection, *Refurbishment*, will be published by Ward Wood in 2011.

www.greyhenpress.com